Eras of the Heart
ISBN: 978-1-329-06220-7
Imprint/Publisher: Lulu.com
Copyright License: All Rights Reserved - Standard Copyright
License
Copyright Holder: Anna Richards
Copyright Year: 2023
Contributors: By (author) Anna Richards

Eras of the Heart

By Anna Richards

Table of Contents

Dedication

For the other depressed missionary kids.

Goals Unfolded in my Suspicious, Hopeful Head

Or, I Keep Trying to Figure Out What I Want

Publicly Processing

Some things I say because
I never heard anyone say that
or I never heard it like it was
an idea I didn't actually have
to understand or comprehend–
just still my mind and ponder at.

Gathered In

Pray over me until there are no lies left
uncover me, and look past the death–
depth cried out to depth and found you,
brought you here to quiet avenues
where I could speak in hesitant tones
be listened to by wiser, older
ears who hear and take me in,
grab me by the spirit and hasten
to gently counsel
to love, love
in accordance with Spirit given from above.

Older, Wiser

I suppose that as I grow
I am becoming something
bigger than the part my heart had once surrendered
smaller than my inner child had once demanded but
so much more enveloped in love
than any of me had ever imagined.

Autopsy of the Psyche

I spend all this time writing
writing
writing
writing
trying to figure myself out
scratching at the surface
scratching at the hole
scratching into the self until
I have little fragments
dusty clauses and mucky sonnets
explaining me better
than I've ever been able to—
everyone has their assumptions
about the totality of me
but I want them to read this
so that they can finally get it.

Lake Lanier in Therapy

We're poking and prodding
at a dam to keep history
at bay, and there's a town
under all that water
that I'm scared to uncover
for fear of the graveyard
it's bound to have become–
people keep trying
to swim in those waters,
but they're filled with
relationship corpses
and foundations I
used to call home.

All the Ailments Paining Me

Or, the Ugliest Inflictions and their Matching Defenses

Rotten Depths Deeply Maintained

Whole—I got used to polluted holes
filled with sludge and murky oil,
spent so long avoiding them
or peeking over the edge on tiptoes
then dipping my feet in and wondering
'how deep does this one go?'

I wish they were trenches
watery drop-offs with immense fish
monstrous creatures with glow sticks
and then I'd have more life in me

I think that once there were coral reefs
shallow and vibrant, and that's what you see
when you think of me at my peak
but now my hands are full of death
I'd shovel it out 'till there's nothing left
but I'm scared of the pits it'll leave behind

can't grow reefs that deep
so what'll it be?

and what about my filthy hands?
after I handled all that murk
I could cut them off, and fashion new ones
prosthetics that don't remember violence
and mistrust, only kindness
there's enough trash in the holes
in the spoiled wells to build them
and with them, I suppose I must
invent a new pair of feet
after I dipped the old ones in
they'll have to go, have to leave
with a mind of their own, they'll walk away
and if I'm losing my mind
it'll drag along my spinal cord
can't use the new shoes
until I chain link a new back bone
as for a brain, I'll manage without it
my heart is still heavy, it'll work in place
until I grow myself a new one

brains can take a while.

I'll stop contributing until then
just donate my heart's aches
until they're mystifying enough to wile you
until my pain is an exhibit for admirers
until you're looking at how I feel
and not how it actually is because
I know
I know
I know
that my heart is easily wooed by lies
let it burn, it is fireproof, I've tested it before
with a sober mind to judge it
let me burn until I'm all
a bunch of parts guided by a heart
waiting to grow new flesh
burn away the partial knowledge
until there's only the bones of hard belief

the things that stayed in my chest
beating loud and clear in the depths
the truth that I know with all of me
not just a rotten brain, or hands, or feet.

Dead Ends

I think my internal organs and each one of my limbs
are striking up minor chords like a thousand lamenting hymns
and my chest, so tightly bound, is now forcing me to feel
all the grief that I left buried in my skull trying to kill

'cause if you bury something alive, it's bound to come back worse
puts you down to bed the way you loaded it into the hearse
I never wanna wake up again, I never wanna put more weight
on the feet that carried me until the sun set too late

the night is cold and dark, and the moon is new again
I cannot see it anymore, there's no connection left.

It's only survival instincts if everyone is a predator—

I'm scared that I will be too weak
and you'll finally realize what a burden
I am to have around
there will always be messes with me
and I can be the one to clean them up
but you'll be there for the smell
as I rise from my weary lump
to gather the vomit and ashes and blood
that follow me like a trail of breadcrumbs
when I'm lurching from my worst

let me hide away
and only come out with a smile
and eloquent words to describe my pain
after it's done debilitating me.

Creating a Case Study

Recognition arrives in the emptiness
when the symptoms of stress quiet down
and the bereaved soul has no breath left
to shout
to sob
to run away
and I'm too tired to eat or breathe or drink
or shower or tidy up or think

so I just sit and hold hands with numbness
and I remember that bile's source is anxiety
and breathlessness comes from heartbreak
and a weak appetite means that what I want
is not easily available for consumption.

Incomplete

Screaming at my self, sustained under my breath
hanging from my neck like identity on a lanyard

"Did you ever learn how to be enough?" is what I said
but every day I kept on falling further from the standard.

Damnation

The gnashing of teeth is a
personal punishment
carried out and suffered
all by myself
my lips and my nails
scraping into me.

Bring Out the Rain

Maybe I love myself the easiest
soaked in the torrential downpour
spine chained the the floor
because I spend the rest of the time
reminding myself the sun still shines
even though I'm freezing cold.

Nostalgia for the Sea

My tears match the ocean for salt
because every time I see a wave they well

up in longing, pining for rising atolls
and my body rocks in time with the swells
of the tide as I lay my head to rest

I'm still waiting to return to the port
and sail away until no land is left
visible in horizon's well-told lore.

The Facade as I Created It

Or, the Person You Used to See was Carefully Designed

A Character

Maybe it's the feeling
of every made-up edge
fluttering and peeling
down around my legs
like a costume I put on
every single day

I venture far beyond
the limits of my stay
and I wander in the wings
of all the world a stage

wishing I were a stagehand
instead of an actress in a rage.

Worthiness Poorly Quantified

I would measure myself
by the pieces of me you affirmed
and the ones you denounced
without a clue as to neutrality
and no unspoken lines to guide me
as they'd all abandoned me
to leave room for socially
useless traits that aided me
in unremarkable ventures like
being more interesting
than anyone else
and expecting them all
to be that consistently competent.

Fortress

There's comfort in a quick defense
and tight walls all around

but no renewal nor intimacy
a stony bed to lie in.

Wearisome Habits

I'm tired of living up to the same compliments
tired of making a home within the confines
of loss and absence and grief and sudden newness
tired of changing soils, and I don't think I'm blooming

I'm not enough for the younger version of myself
who held up under pressure and learned to excel
and I'm not enough for a future of pushing back hell

and I guess that I'm not doing very well.

Anti-Heroic Escape

I've spent years trying to be enough
for the goliath I made you out to be

so long that I covered you up with a mask
while I put on my own domino
as if I could manufacture my sanctification
by means of a secret identity

or heal my hesitant spirit
by running into a blazing inferno

and I wondered why I hated hypocrites
when I was producing so much duplicity.

I Think I'll Leave the Cave

My mind is bleary-eyed,
easy to numb, easily lying
to itself: out of comfort?
As much as anesthetic is comfort
I'm still up at 2
self-medicating on narrative
to stop up my tear ducts
so they never drown me.

I could pull back the curtain
in briefly lasting shifts
slowly uncover the miry pits
but I have to adjust myself
to seeing them.

Here is Who I Have Been, the Person Who Made Me

Or, I Used to Think Too Much About How Much of Me was Left.

Sidewalk Grounded

I find myself losing complacency in my placeless nature
and my eternal guest status slowly loses honorable favor
while devolving and unveiling to reveal a homeless person
except I've never had so simply understandable a label

I'm wary of the rooms I sleep in but half-heartedly possessive
easily shooed out and awfully bitter in the same breath
with long memory and short expectations
but my memory's wearing out and my expectations are stretching

and now I want to stick around.

Wiggle-room

Am I older and wiser

or worn down and weary

my joints overused, so my bones are all scraping
together, they have me hyper-aware of my failings
and I'm so very small and I'm gracelessly fading
just the sum of bad decisions that led me to here

still not sure what it means to be healed
except that healing seems to imply wholeness
and I'm fresh out of lies
so there's space for new growth

but the emptiness tries to cry
out for empty calories or me to vacuum seal
the extra space away
but then I'd lose the breathing room
that gives me go-ahead for dancing.

Jazz Tempo

My identity feels tentatively defined
between ticks of a metronome
before you hit the other side
the strain of an off-beat, soft-spoken lie
and knowing we'll never rediscover home
the sound as I drown or send off a signal
and the moment before echolocation returns abysmal

waiting 'til you understand the moments that you missed.

Fragmented Affection

I invest pieces of my heart into individuals
that is what my love is

because I don't trust myself to keep all safe;
the unfortunate side effect tripping me up

too many pieces missing debilitates me
and 'though I'm always missing pieces
most of them are gathered up

home is where the (majority of the) heart is.

Trust Issues

I stunted myself pretending
so I never actually learned how
to trust You
and I'm looking back
thinking it did more harm than good
wondering how realistic growth would track
along the epithets people've used for me.

Odd Means of Teenage Rebellion, a Few Years Too Late

Materialism feels so much like rebellion
like letting loose and letting people think I'm a helion

flicking rubber bands at every declared 'resilient'
and tired of people thinking I'll snap back into place
I think I'll fill up a room and stare at all the faces
hang them up in my room like posters, I can't replace
the living with the never-alive, but I try to hold space

for those pictures, for knick knacks and fillers
to remind me I have a place.

Timeshare

Chicago feels further away than Nabire,
and it's not been a month, but I'm scared
that I've lost an entire city with the season
the wind changes and my heart races
though we're still sharing two hemispheres
I'm scared that I'll fade away
from the minds of all my distant loves
scared that I never had a foothold
in their minds to begin with.

I have always been somewhat replaceable
in the limits of my mind, dispensable
but every individual I know is
more than they will ever believe, fantastical
so what does that make me?

Art Student

If I could feel myself with an outsider's hands
and pinch my sides with my own ten foreign fingers
would I write happy love songs to be played by a band
or scorn the same flesh within which I must linger?

I'm not much for paints and pencils, but I like them on occasion
spinning clay and carving marble have eluded me thus far
but would I dedicate my simple skills to pointed adulation
of this body I have settled in that some days feels like lard?

Adopted Beliefs

I think some people have to learn how to be loved

or at least I hope that it's common enough
that someday, someone will be so kind as to teach me
again and again, and maybe they'll reach me.

Patchwork Soul

Always I'm carving identity
tentatively trying hand at it
with wood from grafted tree
varnished in honey that sticks
on my too-soft fingertips

I add old garments to my closet
and look at them, wondering
if I can wear them appreciatively
enough to cover old dishonor
from eras long gone and eras barely
over. I poke and prod at this self
because it doesn't belong on shelves
made by bitter hands or angry heads,
but still, I wonder what I make up

and I consider significance
audaciously, oddly, full of anger
lacking kindness for the child
who tried her hand at creating before I could.

Christian Character Award

I used to be so old for my age,
I once won an award for my sanctification

was I spiritually mature or constantly afraid
of being alone when all I'd known was a cage?

The world was so big, and to me, so small
and every corner was quietly haunted
by looks from adults expecting much more
than the standards they had for their own morals

they saw in me purity they wanted to preserve
while tossing my heart into a desert
like it didn't matter so long I leaned on Father

I learned I should trust God and baby the church
because the church as it was put me on pedestal
relied on a child while feeding adults baby food

or maybe they fed on sound doctrine and theology
while nobody expected independent practicality.

I learned how to walk the walk all the way to hating God
because the second I showed weakness I was told
I should think of the way people look at me

I wanted them to look and see
that I was killing myself

I was trying to kill myself in the name of a savior
who had already died for me.

I wanted to be enough.

religious peer pressure

They tell me to stand and sing
as though you are deaf
to the cries of my heart
and it feels like a competition
of volume in the house of the Lord

"This is the day that the Lord has made…"

feels like a weapon against me
and a blade held against my throat
by someone grabbing me from behind.

Silhouetted

I used to be the sun
that only served to show
your shadowy silhouette

so you became a whole person,
and I was just the bright thing

I told her that I wanted to be
more than a bright thing

I wanted to be a person
and so I became.

The Silver Lining as It Peeks

Or, this is Somewhere Between Wandering and Wondering.

Worn In

I like it when the edges of my clothes
are all frayed and ripped and worn through
because it puts me at ease

matching the outside to the inside

then, maybe, people won't expect
a version of me made to suit them
and instead they might create space
to fit the me who is a bit unraveled

a protective embrace to hold me together
rather than a rough handling
for the purpose of patchwork.

Life Against the Dying

I've witnessed glimpses
in untouched creation

years, months, days before corruption
at the hand of greedy man
imminently close to dying
diminishing under cruel dominion

and at the same time I'm craving
to preserve what's remaining

I wonder if there's any way
to dominate the earth in holiness
if it looks as violent as the methods
that scarred the earth in the first place

or if it is insistently gentle

demanding of love-rich study
and a discerning eye for placed beauty
and hands that follow, ever-steady.

New Again

My tree is experiencing new growth
just as I, myself, am allowing new hope
to spring forth within my cynical heart
and I'm chipping away at a brand new start
which lends itself to paler leaves and stems
as the chlorophyll is racing up the limbs

and I am a garden of body and bloom
holding out faith for reflections off the moon.

Golden Glow of Desertion

I remember easy holidays
and the comfortable, singular home
steeped in myth and memories
and never being scared to go, oh

the mangoes, sticky, fallen and bruised
just like my head on the worst of days
stuck in a fog I'm trying to lose
while skyscrapers rise in the golden haze

beautiful, beautiful!

Reunion with an Old Friend

I'm always looking at you expecting
all the vibrant popularity of youth
and I have come to see that we
are not as far removed

from each other as I once believed

both finding our way over obstacles
and through painful growing seasons
made up of monsoons and beating sun
and a million mediocre moments.

Melting

If I poured poured myself out like a drink offering
the blood would drip down to your hands slowly
and I'm scared you won't take this defrosting old soul

but if I set it on fire, the inside would stay cold
frostbitten, freezer-burned edges need miracles.

Perhaps I need to sit in the sun and be warmed
enjoy a whole day while the leaves are turning gold

stretch out on the grass while a friend weighs me down
and let Your love whisper through the tree branch boughs
gentle in my ear, I'd hear, "Rest, my child."

Mistaking Fear for Reverence

Teach me how to love you
a bit more than I used to

as much as I thought I did

or the way I wished that I could quit
all those nights that I spent sobbing
crying, "God, could you still want me?"

oh, teach me how to fall
without both hands braced on the wall
without looking around full of fear
that you will leave me here.

Legion

You are homed in the tombs

cast aside to the cemeteries
like a ghost who is fading away
from memory and humaneness

except there isn't even a headstone
not for you, no bed to lay on
no peace in rest or safety
and you are hopeless, homeless

are you waiting for someone
to ask who you are?
Were you waiting for the savior

or did he take you entirely by surprise
after everyone else had given up
after love had been robbed from you,
how did your body quake in the regaining?

And now he has sent you to your home
which you had lost up 'til this point,
which no one has let you call your own
for all this time, in this tomb;

how do you go back to the place
that scorned you for all that time?
And how do you leave the man
who loved you when no one else did?

But you *can* belong now, so you must
return to the place that was your birthright
(the man gave you to your family
in the first place, so again he blesses them)

did you know, love, that you were created
with blessing to your family in mind
blessing to your place which wasn't ready
for the savior when he came this time?

Ambition

I'm straining against the boundary lines of my old life
self-imposed and un-loathed yet pressurized

I have tracks down my cheeks for the tears on repeat
and they only know one way to go

barely watering my angry soul
racetracks that I'm turning into farm grounds

how do I maintain a summer's growth
when the August rain begins to come and go
like a woman who forgot half the recipe at the store

I'm telling my friends to hold me accountable
for curiosity and losing control

while I try to stop relying on the record in my head
saying, "I should already know, already know."

An Awkward, Slow Procession toward Healing

Or, How Sweet are the Friends Who Nursed Me Back to Health.

gentle

Jesus looks up at me
doesn't demand a risen chin
but lowers himself to hold
my downturned head
taps my cheek with his
calloused carpenter's thumb
and he draws me in
to whisper in my ear

"Beloved, I am with you."

To Church

Sky's white 'n' clouded-over from the downpour
and there's flooding in my community's basements
so church was canceled
but I kept riding the train, all the way
to see the faces I could

the quiet and sturdy remnant of them
were calling each other from sanctuary
I picked up lunch after saying goodbye
and missed the time
we would've had together

I can remember recently
when church made me loud and vibrant
like face paint, like a mask I had to scrape off
for relief at the end of the day

I had always been terrified of exposing myself
but I put on such a show, and they didn't know
the raw part of me is quiet and rambling
unrehearsed and unrefined and vulnerable

shouldn't a person feel the most like themself at church?

I thought church was homey and warm
for everyone else, but not for me
for me it was conscious amplification of all my acceptableness
and diminishment of all my disappointing portions

when the sky was white and cold today
I couldn't wait to get to church
because I wanted to go to that home
all that's left of the mask I once kept
are traces of paint that get washed away
layer by layer in the sink, on Sundays.

Be Like

Love the little children like Jesus draws them in
learn how to be loved like they do, running in
they never look before they leap into the Father's arms
they never try to dry their tears or quiet down their sobs
just run and cry and feel, feel, feel, the Father-Mother's pause.

Lively

Bathed in sunlight, nourished in water
all the wild things are of a mind to squander
their Creator's love, infinite, boundless as it is
poured out easily, flooding the green quickly
until all the meadows and forests and jungles
the savannahs and tundras and so on and so forth
are living testaments to God's goodness.

Raw and Joyful

My throat is delightfully raw
from screaming with my friends
and I'm learning to grow brighter
a bit more me again.

The Kindness of Fat

How kind is it that while my mind was hardening
my body was reaching out and softening

stretch marks like slashes over my womb
feathery-relaxed as I dip my fingers into them
to remind me that this flesh was protecting me
while I was hating every part of it

mind, heart, soul, body
and now when I dive into my despair
there is comforting, squishy skin which for me cares.

Letting Go and Letting God: a Study in Falling

Feeling lighter isn't the easiest thing;
I had more substance in survival mode
when I had all that responsibility.

I carried over my weight
as I lost muscle I was using to carry it
I collapsed under the weight
I'd been priding myself in
when the adrenaline wore off.

There's so much falling involved
in falling in love with God

I used to think myself
above such a clumsy drawl.

Triumphally Made New

Here is a voice
and ears to hear it
whisper for as long as you like
until you cannot help but shout out

"I am healed! Jesus healed me!"

because you're opened up
like a flower in new bloom
like a trumpet with the mute taken out

open up with the joy of healing
from your savior, from your delight!

Conclusion

I have always been hesitant to show the poems I wrote in a healthy place to the people who have loved me the longest. I know how hard it is to maintain a kind sense of self, and I don't want to disappoint people by slipping back into a darker headspace. I have Recurrent Major Depressive Disorder, which means that I am prone to return to my lowest point.

But it is imperative that I record these high moments. I must always remind myself of the Lord's goodness, and of my own ability to experience it. God calls me to a theology of memory, and so I remind myself of God's love in these poems.

Acknowledgements

I have often imagined dedicating a book, and I've always known it would be a difficult task. It's hard to pin down a person or even a limited group who inspired me to this end–to writing, to writing poetry, to writing a book of poetry, to making it public. I can try.

My mom taught me how to read and write, and my dad taught me how to love the two. Mom picked out a program called "Sing, Spell, Read, and Write" as my curriculum, because I was always singing. I often wonder how much of the giftedness she believes I have is the product of her way of love, which is intentional and earnest and always trying to be better than what came before it. Meanwhile, my dad would gather up my brother and I at the end of the day, and read from chapter books to us as part of our night routine. My parents loved my brother and I vividly.

There are so many peers who encouraged my poetry, but a few come to mind as the ones who believed I could turn it from a rare hobby into an everyday meditation. Brian Bastos challenged me to begin writing creatively several times a week. A counselor, Doxa Zannou, gave me homework prompts to journal about, and she accepted that journaling in the form of my poetry. Lexi Scanlan once stayed on a video call with me for several hours, and we each read an exhaustive compilation of our respective work to each other.

Nimurungi Marvel published *Let the L's be Known* last year. Since even before that, she would tease me and ask when I would write my own book–here it is, Marvel. I hope you like it.

Lizzy Sullivan came into my life at an odd point. She inspired more honesty from me than anyone else by the way that she is honest. If not for her, I would not have been able to be so confident in the value of what I have to say in poetry. Furthermore, she was one of my most helpful editors.

Hannah McMahan has been so steady in my life. One of my greatest fears is being forgotten, and she consistently makes me feel thought of. She also helped me in the early stages of writing and formatting.

It's hard to define all the ways my brother influenced this end result. He was vital in the editing process, and as a significant inspiration, and he is my brother–he's been here with me in more of my pain and joy than any other person. At one point of drafting, I made him sit in an airport with me, an hour before either of our flights would board, and I made him read every poem I had written thus far. There was a point when he apologized to me–it's so strange and incredible to talk about pain with my brother. I forgave him, because I had already forgiven him. I apologized to him, too.

The last section of this is about healing. God is my healer, and my church—Missio Dei, in Albany Park—those people were the easily inspired, the quickly moving people among whom I realized God loved me gently.

And I am so thankful for the missionary kids who helped me make sense of my life when I could not.